Engineering Education and Practice in the United States

Engineering Technology Education

Panel on Technology Education
Subcommittee on Engineering Educational Systems
Committee on the Education and Utilization of the Engineer
Commission on Engineering and Technical Systems
National Research Council

NATIONAL ACADEMY PRESS
Washington, D.C. 1985

NATIONAL ACADEMY PRESS 2101 Constitution Ave., NW Washington, DC 20418

NOTICE: The project that is the subject of this report was approved by the Governing Board of the National Research Council, whose members are drawn from the councils of the National Academy of Sciences, the National Academy of Engineering, and the Institute of Medicine. The members of the committee responsible for the report were chosen for their special competences and with regard for appropriate balance.

This report has been reviewed by a group other than the authors according to procedures approved by a Report Review Committee consisting of members of the National Academy of Sciences, the National Academy of Engineering, and the Institute of Medicine.

The National Research Council was established by the National Academy of Sciences in 1916 to associate the broad community of science and technology with the Academy's purposes of furthering knowledge and advising the federal government. The Council operates in accordance with general policies determined by the Academy under the authority of its congressional charter of 1863, which establishes the Academy as a private, nonprofit, self-governing membership corporation. The Council has become the principal operating agency of both the National Academy of Sciences and the National Academy of Engineering in the conduct of their services to the government, the public, and the scientific and engineering communities. It is administered jointly by both Academies and the Institute of Medicine. The National Academy of Engineering and the Institute of Medicine were established in 1964 and 1970, respectively, under the charter of the National Academy of Sciences.

Support for this work has been provided by the National Science Foundation, the Department of the Air Force, the Department of the Army, the Department of Energy, the Department of the Navy, and the National Aeronautics and Space Administration. Additionally, assistance has been provided through grants from the Eastman Kodak Company, Exxon Corporation, the General Electric Company, the IBM Corporation, the Lockheed Corporation, the Monsanto Company, and the Sloan Foundation.

Library of Congress Catalog Card Number 85-62838
ISBN 0-309-03632-1

Printed in the United States of America

Preface

The Panel on Technology Education was one of four panels established by the Committee on the Education and Utilization of the Engineer to investigate educational aspects of the preparation of engineers in the United States. Although its membership was limited, the panel sought to provide as broad a base of experience and expertise as possible. Panel members were drawn from the fields of civil, electrical, and mechanical engineering. Their backgrounds included experience with large and small institutions, both state-supported and independent, and with programs that ranged from two-year curriculum through graduate study. In addition, panel members represented a number of geographic areas, such as the Northeast, the Middle Atlantic states, and the Southwest.

At the beginning of its study, the panel identified a list of topics that it considered to be of primary concern in engineering technology education. This report documents the panel's findings relating to these topics and its recommendations for further action. The study is also intended to provide supporting material for the main report, * to which readers are therefore referred for information in other areas of specific interest. (For further information on educational issues, see also the companion volumes of the other three education panels.)

* *Engineering Education and Practice in the United States: Foundations of Our Techno-Economic Future* (Washington, D.C.: National Academy Press, 1985).

In conclusion, I wish to express my appreciation to the many participants in this study on technology education—the panel members and the staffs of both the National Research Council and the Wentworth Institute of Technology—for their invaluable efforts in collecting and condensing the available material.

EDWARD T. KIRKPATRICK
CHAIRMAN

Panel on Technology Education

EDWARD T. KIRKPATRICK, Chairman; President, Wentworth Institute of Technology
JOHN D. ANTRIM, General Manager, Certification Programs, National Society of Professional Engineers
STEPHEN R. CHESHIER, President, Southern Technical Institute, Marietta, Georgia
RICHARD A. KENYON, Dean, College of Engineering, Rochester Institute of Technology
LAWRENCE J. WOLF, Dean, College of Technology, University of Houston
DONALD TRITSCHLER, Consultant, Shrewsbury, Massachusetts

Committee on the Education and Utilization of the Engineer

JERRIER A. HADDAD, Chairman (IBM, Ret.)
GEORGE S. ANSELL, Dean of Engineering, Rensselaer Polytechnic Institute (now President, Colorado School of Mines)
JORDAN J. BARUCH, President, Jordan J. Baruch Associates
ERICH BLOCH, Vice-President, IBM Corporation (now Director, National Science Foundation)
DENNIS CHAMOT, Associate Director, Department for Professional Employees, AFL/CIO
EDMUND T. CRANCH, President, Worcester Polytechnic Institute
DANIEL C. DRUCKER, Dean of Engineering, University of Illinois at Urbana (now Graduate Research Professor of Engineering Sciences, University of Florida at Gainesville)
FRED W. GARRY, Vice-President, Corporate Engineering and Manufacturing, General Electric Company
JOHN W. GEILS, Director of AAES/ASEE Faculty Shortage Project (AT&T, Ret.)
AARON J. GELLMAN, President, Gellman Research Associates, Inc.
HELEN GOULDNER, Dean, College of Arts and Sciences, Professor of Sociology, University of Delaware
JOHN D. KEMPER, Professor, Department of Mechanical Engineering, University of California at Davis
EDWARD T. KIRKPATRICK, President, Wentworth Institute of Technology

ERNEST S. KUH, Professor of Electrical Engineering and Computer Science, University of California at Berkeley
W. EDWARD LEAR, Executive Director, American Society for Engineering Education
LAWRENCE M. MEAD, JR., Senior Management Consultant (Senior Vice-President, Ret.), Grumman Aerospace Corporation
M. EUGENE MERCHANT, Principal Scientist, Manufacturing Research, Cincinnati Milacron, Inc. (now Director, Advanced Manufacturing Research, Metcut Research Associates, Inc.)
RICHARD J. REDPATH, Vice-President, Ralston Purina Company
FRANCIS E. REESE, Senior Vice-President, Monsanto (now retired)
ROBERT M. SAUNDERS, Professor, School of Engineering, University of California at Irvine (Chairman, Board of Governors, AAES, 1983)
CHARLES E. SCHAFFNER, Executive Vice-President, Syska & Hennessy
JUDITH A. SCHWAN, Assistant Director, Research Labs, Eastman Kodak Company
HAROLD T. SHAPIRO, President, The University of Michigan
MORRIS A. STEINBERG, Vice-President, Science, Lockheed Corporation
DONALD G. WEINERT, Executive Director, National Society of Professional Engineers
SHEILA E. WIDNALL, Professor of Aeronautics and Astronautics, Massachusetts Institute of Technology

Staff

WILLIAM H. MICHAEL, JR., Executive Director
VERNON H. MILES, Staff Officer
AMY JANIK, Administrative Assistant
COURTLAND S. LEWIS, Consultant

Government Liaison

LEWIS G. MAYFIELD, Head, Office of Interdisciplinary Research, National Science Foundation

Contents

Executive Summary

The Panel on Technology Education prepared this report as a part of the overall effort of the National Research Council's Committee on the Education and Utilization of the Engineer. In its investigations, the panel studied a number of aspects of technology education. The technical institute movement was examined, and recent developments were noted. The panel also sought to distinguish between engineering education and engineering technology education, proposing definitions and delineating similarities and differences that might enable better program and curriculum development. Various types of degree programs and other facets of engineering technology education, such as student chapters of associations, special-interest clubs, and cooperative education, were also examined. In addition, the panel considered manpower needs for engineering technology education, the impact of high technology on current and future programs and curricula, and the allocation of resources between the various technical areas of study (e.g., precision measurement, welding, computer hardware, numerically controlled machining, etc.). As a result of its studies, the panel developed a number of recommendations for action to improve engineering technology education. These recommendations are noted in the paragraphs below.

The panel proposed that college faculties and administrations should endorse national efforts to raise high school student achievement levels and subsequently raise college admission requirements for engineering technology programs by adopting more rigorous entry standards. Also, vocational/technical programs in high school and engineering technology programs at the college level should join in efforts to upgrade the curricula, faculty, and facilities at both educational levels. Another proposal was that consortia of educational institutions and industry be formed to improve existing programs and to develop new programs for all to share. An integral part of all such programs should be communication skills: reading, writing, listening, and speaking.

Students should be advised and actively informed about the similarities and differences between engineering and engineering technology. Those students who demonstrate superior ability in two-year engineering technology programs should be encouraged to continue their education by transferring into bachelor's degree programs in either engineering or engineering technology.

Desirable academic and industrial credentials for engineering technology should be identified, and faculty development programs should be sponsored to achieve these standards. In addition, some institutions should accept the challenge of offering graduate education in technologies that will include research in the application and dissemination of technology and faculty should be encouraged to publish their work on these topics.

The panel developed a number of specific recommendations on classes and labs. Semester credit hours for technology programs should range from 16 to 20 hours. Examinations should be given in all courses with interinstitutional cooperation to establish national standards of achievement in basic science and technology courses. As a general rule, the panel recommended that whenever quantity and quality compete, the major focus for change should be on quality.

In addition to these specific technology education recommendations, the panel proposed the following actions on related issues:

- Student chapters of engineering-related associations be encouraged by the associations and faculty sponsors in order to provide students with additional contacts and activities with national societies and their representatives.
- Cooperative education in all of its forms should be expanded through greater industrial, institutional, and governmental support, with faculty-industry linkages being encouraged.
- "Hallmark" programs in engineering technology should be identified, publicized, and supported nationally.
- Appropriate accrediting agencies should play a greater role in efforts to increase the quality of engineering technology programs.

- Students should be prepared for and encouraged to seek technician certification.
- Professional registration or certification of engineering technology faculty should be encouraged.
- Manpower statistics on enrollment, degrees, and salaries should be maintained at the college, state, and national levels.

The panel considered the impact of high technology to be of major importance in engineering technology education. Computers and computer technology should be recognized as one of the most powerful educational delivery systems now available and applied in all academic programs in engineering technology. There should also be greater incentives for faculty to use modern educational technologies in teaching.

Finally, the panel considered the way institutions allocate their resources to the various areas of engineering technology. The following recommendations were developed:

- Institutions should plan to develop a limited number of "centers of emphasis" in subspecialties.
- Continuing efforts should be made to upgrade laboratories and shops, recognizing the importance they play in the education of engineering technicians and technologists.
- Linkages with industry should be developed to share specialized laboratory and shop facilities, both in industry and on the campus.

1

The History of Technical Institutes

In 1956, Smith and Lipsett [1] stated that "although the present day technical institutes can trace their history back to the founding of the Ohio Mechanics Institute in 1828, the past twenty-five years have undoubtedly seen a more rapid development of the technical institute movement than any other quarter century." Today, the same statement holds true, but for different reasons.

From 1931 to 1956, the most significant developments in the growth of technical institutes included the Wickenden study conducted for the Society for the Promotion of Engineering Education (SPEE); the accreditation of technical institute curricula by the Engineers Council for Professional Development (ECPD); the establishment of the Technical Institute Division of the American Society for Engineering Education; the accumulation of a growing body of literature on the technical institute movement; the granting of the associate's degree for two-year technical institute programs; and the establishment of the McGraw-Hill Award to outstanding technical institute educators.

One of the major benefits of these efforts was the collection of data on the current status of technical institutes, allowing educators and practitioners to document growth and determine future directions. For example, only 9 of the 34 institutions listed in the 1931 SPEE study were predominantly technical institutes. The others were regular degree-granting colleges or universities or "industrial schools of mixed character." However, the Seventh Annual Survey of Technical Insti tutes, conducted in January 1951 by Smith and Lipsett, showed a major increase in the numbers of technical institutes:

- State and municipal—22
- Privately endowed—12
- Extension divisions of colleges and universities—12
- Proprietary institutions—22
- YMCA schools—2

Since 1956 the technical institute movement has continued to grow. The most significant developments include the offering of engineering technology programs in the expanding community college movement, the "vacuum" created by engineering colleges as they tend to shift toward engineering science, the introduction of four-year bachelor's degree programs, and the certification of technicians. (A history of the development of the baccalaureate degree in engineering technology can be found in the dissertation by Mallonee. [2]) Four specific areas of development—accreditation, the roles of professional associations and of junior colleges, and continued data collection—are highlighted below.

ACCREDITATION

ECPD inaugurated its accreditation activities for engineering programs in 1932. In 1945 its accreditation of associate degree programs began with visitations to the Bliss Electrical School and Capital Radio Engineering Institute, both in Washington, D.C., and Wentworth Institute of Technology in Boston. Accreditation of baccalaureate engineering technology programs began in 1967 with a Brigham Young University program. The fifty-first annual meeting of the Accreditation Board for Engineering and Technology (the successor to ECPD) reported that in 1983 there were 195 institutions with 731 programs being accredited. [3]

ASSOCIATIONS

The Technical Institute Division (the name was changed to the Engineering Technology Division in 1971) of the American Society for Engineering Education (ASEE) met for the first time in 1941. [4] ASEE also established the Technical Institute Council (now the Engineering Technology College Council) in 1962, as a parallel organization to the Engineering College Council primarily for administrators in engineering technology. A review of the ASEE's annual program shows that engineering technology educators and engineering educators have arranged simultaneous programs of about equal magnitude. The membership of ASEE is now approximately 10,000; 2,800 have identified engineering technology education as their main interest.

The Engineering Technology Leadership Institute (ETLI) was established in 1976 and subsequently has met annually to provide leadership development programs to engineering technology faculty and administrators. The three groups, the Engineering Technology Division (for faculty), the Engineering Technology College Council (ETCC) (for institutional representatives), and the Engineering Technology Leadership Institute have issues and members in common. Many concurrent cooperative activities are now planned, and a study group is considering the merits of merging ETCC and ETLI.

DEVELOPMENT OF THE JUNIOR COLLEGE.

Junior colleges originally were established to offer primarily two-year terminal programs to a large proportion of their students. Currently, however, many junior college programs are similar to the first two years of a four-year liberal arts program, and ample evidence indicates good articulation for transfer to four-year institutions for qualified students. Junior colleges have recognized the need to prepare youth for industry, and some now offer three types of technology related programs: (a) two-year terminal programs in engineering technology, (b) two-year programs designed as the first two years of engineering programs, and (c) two-year programs in industrial technology.

Programs designed primarily as the first two years of engineering education are reasonably well defined. But problems of definition exist for programs in engineering technology and industrial technology. These definition issues cause continuing confusion in the categorization and reporting of enrollments and degrees in the three types of programs at both junior colleges and technical institutes.

CONTINUED DATA COLLECTION

Through the efforts of the Engineering Technology College Council of ASEE, a network of state representatives has been established to report the names of institutions and their programs in engineering technology. Using this network and through a cooperative effort with the Engineering Manpower Commission, more complete enrollment and degree data can be obtained from the institutions to provide information on the current status of the technical institutes and of technology education.

2

Engineering Technology and Industrial Technology

DEFINITIONS

The industrial technology graduate is a professional with a broad technical and managerial background in a variety of disciplines related to industry. The engineering technology graduate has the professional skills to apply scientific and engineering knowledge to specific problems in the laboratory or in the field. Although the difference between engineering, engineering technology, and industrial technology is clear to the practitioners of each, there are no universally accepted definitions. The Accreditation Board for Engineering and Technology (ABET) currently uses the following definitions:

Engineering is the profession in which a knowledge of the mathematical and natural sciences gained by study, experience, and practice is applied with judgment to develop ways to utilize, economically, the materials and forces of nature for the benefit of mankind.

Engineering technology is that part of the technological field which requires the application of scientific and engineering knowledge and methods combined with technical skills in support of engineering activities; it lies in the occupational spectrum between the craftsman and the engineer at the end of the spectrum closest to the engineer.

The 1979 report of the Engineer Team Definitions Committee of the Engineers' Council for Professional Development (ECPD), ABET's predecessor, included descriptions of the roles and responsibilities of the engineering technician, the engineering technologist, and the engineer. But these descriptions have not received the exposure that the definitions of the two professions have received. Other engineering organizations and groups, such as the American Society for Engineering Education (ASEE) and the National Society of Professional Engineers (NSPE), have discussed the need for better definitions, but they have not produced new and more acceptable ones.

In addition to the practitioners' problem of agreeing on an ideal definition of engineering technology, there is also the problem of differentiating engineering technology from industrial technology. ABET distinguishes industrial technology from engineering technology by identifying differences in the educational programs. ABET's October 29, 1982, Criteria for Accrediting Programs in Engineering Technology state:

Briefly, the differences between educational programs in engineering technology and industrial technology include type of faculty, use of facilities, mathematics, and science sequence content and degree of specialization. More faculty members with professional educational backgrounds appear to staff the present industrial technology programs, whereas a larger number with engineering or technological backgrounds staff the engineering technology programs.

The National Association of Industrial Technology (NAIT), which accredits industrial technology programs, defines the area as follows:

Industrial technology is a profession which requires education and experience necessary to understand and apply technological and managerial sciences to industry. Formal education for such a career is a management-oriented technical curriculum built upon a balanced program of studies in a variety of disciplines related to industry. Included are knowledge and understanding of materials and production processes, principles of distribution, and concepts of industrial management and human relations; experiences in communication skills, humanities and social sciences; and a proficiency level in the physical sciences, mathematics, design, and technical skills to permit the graduate to resolve technical-managerial and production problems.

The graduate may specialize in a professional field such as manufacturing, quality control, industrial marketing, transportation or construction. Typical areas include advanced material technology, industrial processes, automated computerized systems, production planning and control, industrial methods and control, construction project management, plant facility and management, safety, cost analysis and control, product effectiveness and industrial management.

An apparent difference between the definition ABET uses for engineering technology and the definition NAIT uses for industrial technol ogy is that NAIT has chosen to include in its definition the education an industrial technologist receives and the type of work that will normally be done by a graduate. The National Institute for Certification in Engineering Technologies (NICET)[5] uses the following descriptions to identify engineering technicians and engineering technologists:

An "engineering technician" is one who, in support of engineers or scientists, can carry out in a responsible manner either proven techniques, known to those who are technically expert in a particular technology, or those techniques especially prescribed by engineers.

Performance as an engineering technician requires the application of principles, methods, and techniques appropriate to a field of technology, combined with practical knowledge of the construction, application, properties, operation, and limitations of engineering systems, processes, structures, machinery, devices or material, and, as required, related manual crafts, instrumental, mathematical, or graphic skills.

Under professional direction, an engineering technician analyzes and solves technological problems, prepares formal reports on experiments, tests, and other projects, or carries out functions such as drafting, surveying, designing, technical sales, advising consumers, technical writing, teaching, or training. The education of an engineering technician places great emphasis on mathematics and applied physics with intensive laboratory work in which the technician develops practical knowledge and skills. Technicians differ from craftsmen in the extent of their knowledge of engineering theory and methods, and they differ from engineers by reason of their more specialized technical background and skills.

The "engineering technologist" is qualified to practice engineering technology by reason of having the knowledge and the ability to apply well-established mathematical, physical science, and engineering principles and methods of technological problem-solving which were acquired by engineering technology education and engineering technology experience. The engineering technologist will usually have earned a baccalaureate degree in engineering technology or gained considerable technical experience on the job.

The technologist is a member of the engineering team which will normally include technicians and engineers and, for special projects, may include scientists, craftsmen, and other specialists. The configuration of technical personnel possessing complementary capabilities that facilitate the engineering process is, by necessity, peculiar to each situation. The technologist is expected to have a thorough knowledge of the equipment, applications, and established state-of-the-art design and problem solving methods in a particular field.

An analogy. In efforts to compare engineering and engineering technology, various analogies can be made to show that each operates at a high level of professionalism, competence, and reward. Engineering technology is to engineering as aircraft flight captains are to aircraft designers. In society these two activities would be judged as relatively equivalent, but each performs a different function.

SECONDARY SCHOOL PREPARATION

The specific courses and levels of achievement required in high school for engineering and engineering technology are essentially the same. In addition, mathematics and physics provide the intellectual bases for both these fields. The attempts of local, state, and federal groups to improve academic achievement in the public school system will result ultimately in better work by students at the college level. College faculties are gratified to see the "old standards" for high school graduation being reinstated, because many of the resources now being used for high school level remedial work can be used instead for college level studies. Thus, college entry levels would be raised as a consequence of higher achievement by students in the high schools.

Although most of the attention in evaluative studies of high school education has been directed toward mathematics, science, and the liberal arts, it is clear that there must be a parallel concern for quality in vocational/technical studies. The assistance given to high schools by colleges and universities should include efforts by institutions specializing in engineering and technology. Those efforts could include such mechanisms as curricula review committees, guest lectures, and field trips by high school students to the laboratories and shops of nearby colleges.

RECOMMENDATIONS.

1. College faculties and administrations should endorse national efforts to raise high school student achievement levels and subsequently raise college admission requirements for engineering technology programs by adopting more rigorous entry standards.
2. Vocational/technical programs in high school and engineering technology programs at the college level should join in efforts to upgrade the curricula, faculty, and facilities at both educational levels.

3

Engineering Technology and Engineering

Engineering and engineering technology are closely related, and initially they appeal to people with similar interests and backgrounds. [6,7] Both are rooted in the basic sciences and both proceed from a study of the sciences to applications in modern technologies. Practitioners of both careers work in the same types of business and industrial environments, often side by side and often doing similar work on the same projects.

SIMILARITIES

A casual look at the curriculum of the four-year technologist and that of the four-year engineering student in the same field (for example, electrical engineering and electrical engineering technology) shows a similar number of total credit hours required to complete the baccalaureate and congruence in the names and order of the courses in each. In the case of mechanical engineering and mechanical engineering technology students, [8] each studies statics, dynamics, thermodynamics, machine design, physics, chemistry, calculus, differential equations, manufacturing processes, and electrical circuits; in addition, each pursues a basic program in the humanities and social sciences. As is shown later, however, although the names of the technical courses are similar, the actual offerings differ because they use different mathematics and science as prerequisites.

In some schools that have both engineering and technology courses of study, these programs are under the budgetary and managerial supervision of the same dean. Students from both areas may find themselves in the same classroom at the same time taking the same nontechnical course. And both use the same laboratories.

At graduation it is not unusual for a prospective employer interviewing on campus to talk to students from engineering and from technology programs about the same job openings. For some jobs, computer science, physics, and mathematics majors are also considered. In other words, the new technologist, the new engineer, and the science major compete for the same job, often at the same salary. About 80 percent of the engineering graduates and 60 percent of the technology graduates have "engineer" in their job titles.

Thirty-six percent of engineering graduates pursue graduate study (for an average of 1.6 years), as do 18 percent of technology graduates (for an average of 1.4 years). In some graduate programs, such as the Master of Business Administration, graduates from technology and engineering curricula are viewed as being similar; they are perceived as only modestly different when applying to some engineering graduate schools. Other institutions, however, consider the two types of graduates separately when reviewing graduate applications.

Likewise, in some states, graduates of Bachelor of Science in Engineering and Bachelor of Engineering Technology programs, when both are accredited by ABET, sit for the Intern Engineer and Professional Engineer examinations as equals. In many jurisdictions, however, obtaining the PE certification is difficult if not impossible for the B.E.T. graduate, although the technologist may become certified as possessing specific skills (e.g., safety inspector or tool designer).

DIFFERENCES

Although the overall pool of potential students for engineering and technology programs may appear to be homogeneous, the sensitive counselor will notice some significant differences in aptitude and attitude that emerge to differentiate the two groups of students. Those interested in the "why" rather than the "how" of a technological phenomenon will generally tend toward engineering, as will those who are drawn to the abstract and the theoretical; those who prefer to build and operate what was planned may favor the program in technology. [9]

The areas of research, development, and advanced design are more the interests of the engineer, while the business of manufacturing, testing, inspection, quality control, plant operation, and the like more often appeal to the technologist. The engineer develops new procedures for use in the future; the technologist applies this knowledge to operations, equipment components, and routine maintenance procedures. There are no hard and fixed boundaries, however, and both the engineer and the technologist can be found in all areas, though generally in quite different proportions.

Close examination of the curricula for the two fields shows that they differ. Although both require exposure to the basic sciences, for the engineering student that exposure is deeper and broader. The engineer requires more chemistry and more physics and uses mathematics in the basic sciences to a greater degree and with greater rigor than does the technologist. Technology students, on the other hand, often take two or three courses to cover essentially the same material that engineering students cover in one course. Here, also, the difference occurs because of the level of study.

The engineering "core" curriculum provides a common language and fundamental base for all engineers; technology disciplines tend to be unique and specialized. Although the basic engineering sciences, such as statics, dynamics, circuits, electronics, controls, thermodynamics, and materials science, are part of both curricula, course contents are more abstract, and more mathematically rigorous for the engineer than they are for the technologist. Design courses for engineering students tend to emphasize systems design and open-ended problem solution rather than component design and standardized techniques. Design for the technologist is more likely to use approaches applicable to current problem situations similar to those used in course work examples.

Throughout the curriculum, the technology student usually spends far more time in laboratory courses than does the engineer and as a result is better suited to and better trained in laboratory technologies. The required curriculum in humanities and social sciences is usually more extensive for the engineering student although this varies considerably with different institutions. The required study in communications (composition and speech) is probably about the same for both the engineering and the technology student. The number of skill-type technical courses is greater for the technologist than the engineer.

Upon graduation, the engineering graduate who seeks immediate employment may need a period of on-the-job training that draws on a capacity for professional development and continuing self-education. Many engineers move into management positions. The technologist most often moves into a supervisory position.

In recent years, during the same period that the B.E.T. has come to prominence, the engineering curriculum has been evolving both to prepare the graduate for immediate employment in the world of engineering and equip him or her to proceed directly to graduate school for further engineering study at the M.S. and Ph.D. levels. (Perhaps one reason for the rapid growth of undergraduate technology programs has been that engineering curricula have become more theoretical and more oriented toward graduate school than business and industry would like.) The designers of the B.E.T. program assume that the vast majority of graduates will go directly from school to industry. As a result the development of graduate work in technology is still a somewhat controversial subject, and the number of such programs is small by comparison to engineering graduate programs.

The organization of the American Society for Engineering Education (ASEE) includes the Engineering Technology College Council (ETCC), composed of 102 regular members and 45 affiliate members. A review of their agendas/minutes of the past few years indicates that a number of discussions have taken place about the advantages of institutions working jointly on curricula development. Wentworth Institute of Technology, with the help of Ford Foundation funding, maintained a library of catalogues and curriculum materials during the 1970s. Currently, efforts are under way to revive this activity as an educational resource center to serve the entire engineering technology community.

Another joint effort is the Engineering Technology Leadership Institute (ETLI), now in its tenth year. This is a loosely organized group that sponsors annual programs for the specific purpose of developing the leadership in those institutions with engineering technology programs. Typically, about 80 institutions participate in the October meeting each year. There is considerable overlap in the memberships of ETCC and ETLI, and discussions are continuing on how the two organizations might join and still preserve the essential objectives of both.

A third group, the Engineering Technology Division (ETD) of ASEE, presents programs of interest to engineering technology faculty. Many of the programs are about curriculum development.

TRANSFER OPPORTUNITIES

Despite the similarities of engineering and engineering technology curricula, and with the exception of a few institutions, there is little transferability of credit between the two programs, even in the same generic discipline, after a student has gone beyond the first year or so in either program. Such lack of transferability is perhaps a consequence of and evidence that the two programs are actually separate and distinct. The student who after a year or two finds that he or she should really be in the other discipline can find few programs that build efficiently on what has already been learned. One such program is Rochester Institute of Technology's Transfer Adjustment Schedule. The program permits a graduate of the 2-year electrical technology curriculum who demonstrates superior performance and real aptitude for engineering to make the transfer to electrical engineering with minimum loss of time and credit. In approximately 15 years, the program has produced more than 250 electrical engineering graduates whose first 2 years were spent in electrical technology studies.

RECOMMENDATIONS.

1. Greater emphasis should be placed on the communication skills of reading, writing, listening, and speaking in both technical and non-technical courses.
2. Consortia of educational institutions and industry should be formed to improve existing programs and to develop new programs for all to share.
3. Students should be advised and actively informed about the similarities and differences between engineering and engineering technology.
4. Students who demonstrate superior ability in two-year engineering technology programs should be encouraged to continue their education by transferring into bachelor's degree programs in either engineering or engineering technology.

4

Engineering Technology Education

GRADUATE STUDY

The growth of knowledge in the world of today and the sophistication of its goods and services require that the United States raise its level of technological attainment and increase the ambient level of technical understanding throughout its industrial sector. Engineering and science rely heavily on support personnel. But even more, the technicalization of the production of goods and services increases the demand for technical personnel to apply, repair, and maintain the equipment used for that production. All of these functions are likely to require sophisticated knowledge of hardware and software in the future.

The appropriate educational response to this need for technical sophistication is the development of a master's degree in engineering-related technology. [10,11] Some graduates from baccalaureate programs in technology want more depth in a specific field to provide technical support for continuing advancements in engineering. Such intellectual depths are available only in graduate programs. The personnel prepared through these programs will not only disseminate technology more broadly through the work force, they will also produce needed teachers of engineering technology.

Teacher Preparation

A constraint on the preparation of engineering technology personnel has been the shortage of qualified teachers. Many teachers have come from graduate programs in vocational education. But since vocational education is more concerned with teaching methodology than with technological content, such graduate training has been of limited value for teachers who would remain technologically current. Because engineering generates most technology, the best engineering technology teachers are those prepared in disciplines supported by the engineering societies.

Persons with graduate degrees in engineering are sometimes used for engineering technology education. But the best of them usually are more interested in the generation of technology than in its application and dissemination. In general human resources terms, using individuals with engineering graduate degrees for the education of engineering technology students further reduces the availability of the supply of people qualified to teach engineering. And finally, if engineering technology is to achieve its own identity as a discipline in the future, it must assume the responsibility for developing its own body of knowledge and its own faculties. A debate continues about the notion of engineering technology as a separate body of knowledge by those who feel engineering technology is the application and/or dissemination of existing knowledge that is neither unique nor separate.

Level of Graduate Study

For the several reasons stated earlier, some institutions should accept the task of graduate education in engineering technologies. They should define, through performance, what actually constitutes research in the application and dissemination of technology. Such graduate education should not be a lesser engineering graduate program nor merely a continuation of undergraduate education. Institutions seeking to offer graduate degrees in engineering technology must develop a "graduate school mentality." For example, one problem that must be resolved is admissions. Many engineering technology faculty have become accustomed to the open door philosophy of education in which all who wish to study are admitted. Such an approach, however, would undercut the purposes of graduate education. Institutions offering graduate study must establish rigorous criteria for admission of students to the programs, and for the hiring of graduate faculty, one of which must be an intense interest in contributing to the body of knowledge of engineering technology through publication.

Opinions on the development of graduate degree programs in engineering technology are by no means unanimous, however. There are those who question the need for these programs because traditionally there has been a good match between the aspirations of students at the two-and four-year levels and the needs of industry. It is also uncertain whether universities, governmental agencies, and industry can and will support the high cost of quality graduate education. And finally, there are the questions of "turf": Will graduate education in engineering technology take away some of the resources and uniqueness of traditional engineering programs? This debate will continue just as the debate goes on about which institutions and what disciplines should expand graduate programs in traditional engineering programs.

ASSOCIATE AND BACHELOR'S DEGREE PROGRAMS.

Standardization of Curricula

Faculty generally agree that associate degree programs should prepare students both for immediate employment as technicians as well as for continuing their education in engineering technology. (Such opportunities for transfer may attract better students to associate degree technician programs.) Transfer and employment are sometimes complicated, however, because engineering technology curricula vary greatly in their contents and in the time spent in classes and laboratories. Associate degree technician programs range from 60 to 80 semester hours. Some of these programs require very little formal mathematics and science; others are highly quantitative and science based. Some associate degree programs include very little of the humanities and social sciences; others balance such content with technical courses. Some courses serve specific local industry needs and therefore would not have national interest. Programs that are accredited by the Accreditation Board for Engineering and Technology (ABET) must follow its accreditation guidelines and therefore include prescribed numbers of mathematics, science, humanities/social sciences, and technical courses. In addition, qualitative guidelines are followed, providing a relatively high degree of uniformity in ABET accredited programs.

The lack of standardization in many programs for technicians, however, presents problems for baccalaureate programs designed for transfer students with associate degrees. Some baccalaureate programs do little more than provide nontechnical education at the junior or senior level. Others offer programs balanced between liberal and technical courses that take advantage of the students' maturity. The wide variations in the amount of lab and class time and in the content of engineering technology programs, and the difficulties these variations present to students at all levels, indicate a need for wider agreement on curricula in engineering technology.

Class and Laboratory Hours

Associate degree programs should consist of 64 to 80 semester credit hours; and bachelor's degree programs should require from 128 to 160 credit hours. Establishing such standards should help to achieve some uniformity among programs. Institutions should also establish patterns of program content to accomplish each educational purpose. In this way, study will match the requirements of the next level of work, and students can qualify for further study or perform entry-level industrial assignments without taking additional courses.

Corporations and institutions should promote the Technology Accreditation Commission (TAC) accreditation of engineering technology programs. TAC accreditation offers periodic external review of programs and criteria to ensure at least a minimum of curricular balance and rigor. Furthermore, as a commission within the Accreditation Board for Engineering and Technology (ABET), TAC is in a unique position to develop guidelines that complement engineering education while maintaining the distinction between engineering and technology programs for the benefit of employers and potential students.

For instance, TAC offers the following descriptions of a credit hour in the student's weekly activity during a semester session:

1. one hour in class and two hours of study or work outside class, or
2. two hours in an instrumentation-based lab and one hour of data reduction and report preparation, or
3. three hours in a studio or project laboratory.

TAC also recommends that all science courses and approximately half the technical specialty courses include a laboratory, studio, or project component.

STUDENT CHAPTERS

Two popular ways of introducing undergraduate engineering students to their chosen profession are student memberships in national societies and membership in student chapters that operate at various colleges and universities. Engineering technology students, however, do not have as many opportunities to affiliate with discipline-oriented societies and associations for the following reasons:

- The student member category of membership in a professional association is not always open to the engineering technology student because the eligibility requirement is sometimes written to exclude all but students enrolled in accredited baccalaureate engineering programs.
- Student chapters and clubs are frequently found at institutions with baccalaureate engineering technology programs but are less likely to be found at colleges offering only associate degree engineering technology programs.
- Establishing and maintaining a chapter or club is often dependent on the continuing enthusiasm of a faculty advisor who can interest students in pursuing extracurricular activities.

Some colleges, however, do have organizations of this sort for engineering technology students. One campus of approximately 3,000 full-time students in engineering technology curricula with both associate and baccalaureate programs has student chapters of the American Welding Society, American Society of Civil Engineers, Society of Manufacturing Engineers, and Associated Builders and Contractors. Student clubs include the Radio Club, Model Railroad Club, Solar Energy Club, and Flying Club. [12]

RECOMMENDATIONS

1. Desirable academic and industrial credentials for engineering technology faculty should be identified, and faculty development programs should be sponsored to achieve these standards.
2. Some institutions should accept the challenge of offering graduate education in technologies that will include research in the application and dissemination of such technology.
3. Technology faculty should be encouraged to publish with a focus on the application and dissemination of technology.
4. Examinations should be given in all courses with interinstitutional cooperation to establish national standards of achievement in basic science and technology courses.
5. Semester credit hours for technology programs should range from 16 to 20 hours.

6. Whenever quantity and quality compete, the major focus for change should be on quality.
7. Student chapters of engineering-related associations should be encouraged by the associations and faculty sponsors in order to provide students with additional contacts and activities with national societies and their representatives.

5

Cooperative Education and Engineering Technology.

Although cooperative education began over 75 years ago in the College of Engineering at the University of Cincinnati, only about 2 percent of the nation's 9 million college students participate in cooperative education programs. Approximately 220,000 students and 30,000 employers are involved in cooperative education of many types in virtually all disciplines.

National Commission for Cooperative Education statistics show that cooperative education programs operate in one-third of the colleges and universities in the United States. Colleges offering co-op programs range from junior and community colleges with enrollments of 1,000 or fewer students to large private and state-supported universities with enrollments of 40,000 students or more. Programs vary from school to school: some alternate co-op periods with terms of classes, some operate simultaneous with classes (parallel); some alternate liberal arts with technical subjects; some are credit, some noncredit. Despite their differences, however, all postsecondary cooperative education programs in the United States have a strong common thread: they integrate classroom learning with on-the-job experience related to a student's academic major.

FEDERAL ASSISTANCE

Federal grants have been awarded to college cooperative education programs since 1970 when Title IV-D of the Higher Education Act of

1965 was amended to include co-op learning. Programs are now funded under Title VIII. The types of grants awarded include the following: (1) administrative, given to schools to help start a co-op program or help a smaller program expand; (2) training, distributed geographically to give area schools access to a center for professional training; (3) research; and (4) comprehensive demonstration. Between 1970 and 1978, $75 million was awarded to 845 institutions. During that same period, the number of institutions offering co-op programs increased from 195 to approximately 1,000.

The federal government's support of cooperative education is evident in the 1980 appropriation: in a year of budgetary cutbacks, cooperative education was allotted $15 million. In return for this support, the Carter administration proposed new directions for the program to increase student participation dramatically.

Under the fourth type of grant noted above, the Federal Comprehensive Demonstration Grant, as much as $1 million is given for up to three years to support the nonrecurring costs of making a co-op program comprehensive. That is, colleges either offer cooperative education in all programs of study or they offer it to a majority of eligible students, thus integrating co-op more deeply into their operations and developing innovative programs. The return for the government's investment is a number of models for other colleges across the nation to learn from as they plan their own programs. To date, 36 comprehensive grants have been awarded: 3 in 1980, 11 in 1981, 10 in 1982, and 12 in 1983.

FUTURE FEDERAL FUNDING

Federal support of cooperative education has added significantly to the quality and expansion of programs across the nation. The co-op program currently operates with a ceiling of $20 million. The amount appropriated each year under this $20 million ceiling is designated by Congress, which authorized $14.4 million for 1984 grants. However, current legislation authorizing federal funding of cooperative education runs out September 30, 1985, with the expiration of the Higher Education Act of 1965. To prevent the interruption or demise of the program, supporters of cooperative education in the United States are working to ensure that it is included in the new Higher Education Act. They are also requesting that the ceiling for cooperative grants start at $50 million in 1985 and increase to $100 million in 1989.

A legislative committee of the Cooperative Education Association, together with the National Commission for Cooperative Education, has outlined recommended guidelines for reauthorization of Title VIII. In addition to a request to raise the ceiling for annual funding, the two groups have recommended that Title VIII support strengthening, planning, implementation, and expansion of co-op programs through administrative grants, with substantial funding for a small number of high-quality demonstration projects. The recommendations include special consideration for programs that are involved in unique development efforts with industry and for additional funding that is designed to allow cooperative education to keep pace with technical advances (at present, no equipment purchases are allowed with federal co-op grants). Congressional decisions on federal support will be deciding factors in the potential impact of cooperative education in America.

CO-OP PROGRAMS IN ENGINEERING TECHNOLOGY EDUCATION

Co-op programs have long been important in technical colleges. Work experience carefully planned to relate to a student's curriculum can be a valuable part of any technical academic learning experience. Several colleges (e.g., Northeastern, Rochester Institute of Technology, and Wentworth Institute) require co-op experiences for all of their students at the bachelor's level.

Co-op experiences may be alternating or parallel. The alternating model requires that the student alternate academic terms of work and college; the parallel models involve doing both for a part of each term. The typical alternating program requires about five years of full-time enrollment to complete the baccalaureate degree. Many programs view the co-op experience as being academic, and they grant varying amounts of credit for it. Others view it simply as a beneficial, related experience and grant no credit (some award a certificate).

Co-op agreements are carefully negotiated between the college and the employer to ensure a meaningful sequence of experiences for the student. Onsite visits and interviews are common among the designated faculty, the student, and his employer during the work period. Also, the student usually writes a report summarizing the industrial experiences after each work term. Generally, students stay with the same employer through several (or even all) co-op terms, not only continuity but also a meaningful sequence of increasing responsibilities.

Co-op education appears to be beneficial to both students and employers. A two-way screening for employment can occur with no long-term commitment being required of either party. In addition, it can offer a recruiting mechanism as co-op graduates frequently con tinue with their co-op employer after graduation. As a result, these graduates often enter a firm with a head start in company seniority and fringe benefits, as well as first-hand experience on the job.

CONCERNS FOR THE FUTURE

Several issues of concern seem to surface frequently in any discussion of co-op programs:

- the merits of granting academic credit and how to determine the amount;
- how much experience warrants the awarding of a credential;
- evaluation of a student's co-op performance—by a faculty member or a nonfaculty co-op specialist;
- selection and training of faculty and/or administrative advisors;
- keeping faculty actively supportive and involved;
- advising students concerning the pros and cons of the co-op experience;
- serving nontraditional students (minorities, women, handicapped, foreign);
- whether the alternating or the parallel model is more advantageous to the student;
- how to describe living accommodations and help co-op students find ways to minimize getting "out of sync" with peers;
- whether or not special student fees should be charged;
- whether admission to co-op programs should be selective;
- how the college can identify appropriate resources to support a quality co-op program;
- identification and involvement of new employers;
- how employers can be encouraged to be more supportive of co-op education, and make long-term, meaningful commitments to it;
- how to communicate the advantages of co-op to the various publics; and
- the building of a comprehensive data base to support research on issues in cooperative education.

A national assessment of cooperative education was initiated in 1975 at the request of the Office of Planning, Budgeting, and Evaluation of the U.S. Office of Education. Completed in 1977, the study involved 8,185 respondents affiliated with more than 100 two-and four-year colleges in the United States. The findings[13] of the study include the following:

- Those who participate in cooperative education support it. Institutions with cooperative education programs and employers who hire co-op students expressed strong support and indicated their intention to increase the number of students who would participate.
- Cooperative education contributes significantly to the career preparation of students. More students who enrolled in cooperative education programs, as compared to those who did not, perceived their job skills advancing through their undergraduate program. The findings showed that cooperative education contributes to employment after graduation, with a more direct relationship between college major and full-time, aftergraduation employment and a more direct relationship between current job and career plans.
- Cooperative education is a mechanism for student financial assistance.
- Cooperative education is cost-effective for students.
- Cooperative education is cost-effective for employers.
- Cooperative education constitutes a program cost for institutions of higher education. The study showed that the most important reasons for supporting cooperative education were its potential for integrating academic and career development and for developing student motivation.
- Title IV-D of the Higher Education Act has made a significant contribution to the national expansion of cooperative education. As of 1977, approximately 700 programs had been planned, implemented, strengthened, or expanded as a direct result of Title IV-D (now Title VIII) grants.
- It was a sound legislative decision to support cooperative education through direct grants to institutions rather than as additional scholarship or loan monies to students or as subsidies to cooperative education employers.
- The federal investment of Title IV-D (now Title VIII) is more cost-effective than the federal student loan program.
- The future prospects for the national expansion of cooperative education are good. The saturation point of student, institution, or employer participation in cooperative education has not been reached. Two percent of students enrolled in higher education, about one-third of the nation's higher education institutions, and approximately 30,000 employers are involved in cooperative education. The incentives of expansion are far greater than its deterrents, though more adequate and persuasive information about cooperative education is needed.

The Endicott Report, published each year by Northwestern University's Placement Office, asked employers what they might change to improve technical college programs. Their responses, in order of frequency, were as follows: (1) a hands-on approach with more co-op and work experiences, (2) improved communication skills, (3) less emphasis on research and design, (4) closer ties to industry, and (5) more faculty with industrial experience. These preferences relate strongly to the purpose of engineering technology education, but in addition, items 1 and 4 support the merits of cooperative education.

RECOMMENDATIONS.

1. Cooperative education in all of its forms should be expanded through greater industrial, institutional, and governmental support.
2. Faculty-industry linkages should be encouraged.

6

Accreditation, Certification, and Licensing

Academic training and work experience are considered key elements in estimating an individual's ability to perform in the workplace. Two indications that minimum standards of quality have been met in educational programs and personal experience are accreditation for the institution and certification/licensing for the individual.

ACCREDITATION AND RECOGNITION OF QUALITY

The recognition bestowed by graduation from an associate or baccalaureate degree engineering technology program represents in part an evaluation of the quality of those entering the profession as engineering technicians or technologists. The value of academic training increases when accreditation from the Technology Accreditation Commission of the Accreditation Board for Engineering and Technology (ABET) establishes that such training meets the minimum criteria for rigor and appropriateness.

Unfortunately, ABET accreditation is not a national requirement. Although most baccalaureate engineering technology programs have received accreditation, the majority of associate degree programs have not sought accreditation because of its cost and their inability to meet curricular content and faculty accreditation criteria.

LICENSING AND CERTIFICATION

A separate issue involves recognition of the qualifications of the technician or technologist to perform as an employee. Such recognition is available through certification and registration. Licensing and registration are carried out by the individual state governments and are sometimes restricted to those who qualify as engineers. There is no similar process for technicians and technologists, although in some states technicians, and particularly technologists, can be registered as professional engineers. However, the requirements for registration limit the number who can become registered. Certification is a credential that is available to many technicians and technologists, although it normally does not carry the legal status that is associated with registration.

Certification is offered by a number of organizations and is available on a voluntary basis to those who feel they meet the criteria that have been established. The certifications available are usually in a specialty of concern to a professional society or association. They certify that certain members have acquired a specific level of expertise through education and experience. The only nationally applicable certifications that are not tied directly to the needs of individual organizations are the technician and technologist certifications available from the National Institute for Certification in Engineering Technologies (NICET).[5] NICET limits itself to serving as an examining body to evaluate the qualifications of those who voluntarily apply for certification in one of its many programs in a large number of recognized engineering disciplines.

Recently, there has been increased interest in using certification to establish that an individual has the necessary education and work experience to perform specific job tasks. This increased interest is changing the importance of certification from that of a credential desired by an individual for purely personal reasons to that of a credential needed by an individual to obtain employment or to retain a particular job position.

RECOMMENDATIONS

1. "Hallmark" programs in engineering technology should be identified, publicized, and supported nationally.
2. Appropriate accrediting agencies should play a greater role in efforts to increase the quality of engineering technology programs.
3. Students should be prepared for and encouraged to seek technician certification.
4. Professional registration of engineering technology faculty should be encouraged.

7

Manpower Considerations.

The primary source of technician manpower data is the Engineering Manpower Commission (EMC), which conducts annual surveys of educational institutions to obtain data on programs, enrollment, and degrees granted. The annual reports of the Accreditation Board for Engineering and Technology (ABET) also list information on institutions and programs. In addition, employers are surveyed to obtain data on salaries and future demand.

Although EMC uses common definitions, the application of these definitions by officials in the reporting institutions varies. Furthermore, the numbers of institutions reporting vary considerably from one reporting period to the next. Nevertheless, the EMC data are the most extensive available and serve to indicate national trends.

ENROLLMENT

The number of reporting technical institutes increased from 44 to 69 in the surveys conducted by Smith and Lipsett from 1945 to 1955. Enrollment of full-time day students increased from 8,721 to 26,766, of which 10.6 percent (2,837) were enrolled in technology programs. More recently, EMC records show that the number of institutions reporting technology enrollments alone has increased each year—from 44 in 1968 to 166 in 1980. Enrollment in the same period has increased from 23,597 in 1968 to a peak of 65,677 in 1977.

DEGREES

Associate degree data show that there has been an increase of 136.3 percent (from 30,172 to 71,288) in the number of associate degrees awarded from 1971 to 1979. For the same period, the number of baccalaureate degrees increased from 5,148 to 9,355.

INSTITUTIONS AND PROGRAMS

The 51st Annual Report of the Accreditation Board for Engineering and Technology[3] shows that 195 institutions have 731 accredited programs in the categories shown in Table 1. Table 2 presents the historic

TABLE 1 Status of Engineering Technology Programs, by Program Area and Level as of October 1983

	Accredited Programs		
Program Area	Associate	Bachelor's	Total
Aeronautical	4	5	9
Air conditioning	6	1	7
Architectural	25	6	31
Automotive	1	0	1
Bioengineering technology	3	3	6
Chemical	12	0	12
Civil and construction	71	47	118
Computer	13	8	21
Drafting and design	14	5	19
Electrical and Electronic	149	78	227
Electromechanical	8	2	10
Engineering technology (general)	0	4	4
Environmental	2	8	10
Industrial engineering technology	15	7	22
Manufacturing	7	18	25
Marine	0	1	1
Mechanical	95	59	154
Metallurgical	2	1	3
Mining	6	3	9
Nuclear	3	0	3
Petroleum	1	1	2
Surveying	9	1	10
Other	14	13	27
Totals	460	271	731

SOURCE: *Fifty-first Annual Report of the Accreditation Board for Engineering and Technology* (New York: September 30, 1983).

TABLE 2 Historical Growth of Accredited Engineering Technology Programs

	Associate		Baccalaureate		Total	
Year	Institutions	Programs	Institutions	Programs	Institutions[a]	Programs
1946	3	7	—	—	3	7
1951	22	62	—	—	22	62
1956	32	95	—	—	32	95
1961	32	116	—	—	32	116
1966	49	164	—	—	49	164
1967	61	193	1	2	61	195
1968	62	194	3	9	63	203
1969	68	222	5	12	69	234
1970	80	257	12	27	82	284
1971	85	272	17	41	92	313
1972	94	299	19	46	101	345
1973	98	315	29	81	110	396
1974	100	322	36	102	117	424
1975	103	324	45	121	128	445
1976	111	344	57	150	139	494
1977	117	377	62	155	149	532
1978	121	387	67	178	159	565
1979	123	390	70	189	166	579
1980	132	416	83	221	185	637
1981	136	434	88	242	188	676
1982	140	447	91	257	192	704
1983	142	460	91	271	195	731

[a] Some institutions have both associate and baccalaureate degree programs and are only included once in the total for any one year.
SOURCE: *Fifty-first Annual Report of the Accreditation Board for Engineering and Technology* (New York: September 30, 1983).

development of the associate and baccalaureate programs in engineering technology. In addition to the accredited programs in engineering technology, there are other programs for which procedures for accreditation have not been completed. The concomitant development in enrollment is presented in Table 3, taken from the Engineering Manpower Commission[14] published historical summary.

While it must be assumed that the Higher Education General Information Systems (HEGIS) reports have the required information about programs, enrollments, and degrees, to this date information is not available in summary form for engineering and technology.

A study sponsored by the Ford Foundation and managed by the Council on Post-Secondary Education (COPE) is preparing specifications for institutional statistics. Once standard specifications are formulated, all institutions can maintain statistical data in their computers in the

TABLE 3 Historical Summary of Engineering Technology Programs Accredited by ABET[a]

Engineering Technology Students	1973	1974	1975	1976	1977	1978	1979	1980	1981	1982	1983
First year, full time[b]	22,412	23,348	27,315	28,384	31,558	30,757	18,102	22,127	21,483	14,123	23,995
Second year, full time[b]	13,546	13,232	15,945	18,235	19,566	18,254	10,985	13,302	14,434	11,505	16,828
Other full-time associate degree students	491	1,029	811	896	928	515	455	784	541	221	709
Bachelor of Engineering Technology students, third and later years, full time	6,526	6,868	9,121	10,487	12,490	13,063	8,805	11,542	12,389	11,349	18,719
Total full-time students	42,975	44,477	53,192	58,002	64,542	62,589	38,347	47,755	48,847	37,198	60,251
Total part-time students	12,506	14,180	21,476	19,429	14,079	16,949	15,271	17,395	16,639	13,442	24,134
Number of schools[c]	91	96	112	119	135	133	150	166	161	154	161

NOTE: All of the above statistics should be considered approximate because of factors explained in the text.

[a]Data up to and including 1978 represent all enrollments in schools with at least one engineering technology curriculum accredited by the Accreditation Board for Engineering and Technology at the time of the survey. Data for 1979, which first used the new format, identify enrollments in engineering technology *programs* accredited by ABET. All figures indicate enrollments in the fall of each year.

[b]Includes students in both associate and bachelor's degree programs for these years.

[c]Schools with at least one curriculum accredited by ABET. The Pennsylvania State University Commonwealth campuses are counted as one institution.

SOURCE: *Engineering and Technology Enrollments. Part II: Technology* (Engineering Manpower Commission of the American Association of Engineering Societies, Inc., Fall 1983).

required format. Providing institutions are willing to cooperate, it would then be possible for an interrogating computer to gain the information needed for national statistics without employing survey forms.

RECOMMENDATION

Manpower statistics on enrollment, degrees, and salaries should be maintained at the college, state, and national levels.

8

The Impact of High Technology.

Engineering technology programs are equipment intensive. And because the discipline requires that laboratories be devoted in much greater proportion to current arts and practices than to the verification of fundamental concepts, the equipment must be state of the art. The existence of high technology has therefore raised questions in two broad areas of engineering technology education: the use of equipment as instructional technology and the acquisition and instruction in the use of the equipment itself.

EDUCATIONAL TECHNOLOGY AND HIGH-TECH EQUIPMENT

Seventy years ago, Thomas Edison said: "Books will be obsolete. Scholars will soon be instructed through the eye. It is possible to teach every branch of human knowledge with the motion picture. Our school system will be completely changed in ten years." [15] In the 1960s, a Stanford University report stated: "Ten years from now, television will carry some part of the teaching of the great majority of school children in this nation, and it is also expected that television will make available at home to students of whatever age, a large part of the college curriculum." [16] And in 1972, the Carnegie Commission predicted that by 1980 most colleges and universities would have devised adequate administrative and academic authority and procedures for the encouragement and appropriate utilization of instructional technology. [17]

Clearly, none of these predictions has come true. Although the latest high-tech instructional devices are no longer audiocassettes, movies, or television (now they may be videodisks or personal computers), the issues are still the same. The question seems to be, as Dr. David Berkman of the U.S. Office of Education phrases it: "Is education so immobile as to effectively resist all influence for significant innovation which is not based upon a labor intensive approach?" [18] This traditional labor intensive approach to education is reflected in the fact that only about 4 percent of total educational budgets are for materials, including textbooks.

The use of educational technology seems to depend largely on individual teacher initiative and motivation rather than on how current or capable the available equipment is. Many traditionalists, both faculty and administrators, view instructional technology as a frill.

LACK OF SOFTWARE

With the great proliferation over the years of high-tech instructional hardware at ever diminishing costs, the frustrating underutilization of the equipment seems to be caused by the limitations of available software. Few teachers have the time, expertise, or even interest to develop their own software. If high-tech equipment is to be widely used as educational technology in any curriculum, a wide selection of flexible, high-quality, pedagogically sound software must become available.

If the necessary software becomes available, then clearly the exciting range of high-tech delivery systems can provide a real "mechanical advantage" for the busy and often overworked teacher of engineering technology. Indeed, one could argue that the increased use of high-tech instructional equipment is inevitable as long as the cost of labor continues to rise faster than the cost of technology.

HIGH-TECH LAB EQUIPMENT PROBLEMS

Several questions arise from the problem of teaching the use of high-tech equipment in the laboratory. How does a college identify those new, emerging technologies that need to be taught? Once identified, how are priorities assigned so that curriculum and lab decisions can be made? What other subjects will be deleted or given less emphasis so that new technologies can receive attention? How will equipment be purchased and kept current, once important areas are identified?

One approach to the problem of anticipating trends in equipment might be to maintain a broad, general technical curriculum with a strong emphasis on the fundamentals while dealing with only several indepth specialty areas that can reasonably be kept current. This approach favors providing "survivor skills" and a background to ensure graduates maximum future flexibility with and adaptability to new equipment.

Another approach might be to emphasize the fundamentals but at the same time develop selected laboratory centers of excellence. One example of this method is Georgia's Southern Technical Institute. Realizing that present funding levels would not permit keeping all 55 of its labs at state-of-the-art levels, it established 10 centers of laboratory excellence. The chosen areas had to satisfy several criteria. First, they must be important to Georgia's economy and they must be in fields in which experience with the most advanced equipment was essential for graduate placement. Second, the areas must be those in which the college was already active and had faculty expertise. Finally, they had to be fields for which sources of private and industrial funding were identified. As a result of this program, the institute's 10 high-tech labs allow the college to teach the latest technologies in such fields as satellite communications, automated manufacturing, laser and fiber optics, computer-aided design, and office automation.

Multiple funding sources have been identified for the centers as required by the established criteria. The Satellite Communications Lab, for example, was funded through a major equipment grant ($100,000) from a local industry, a gift of $180,000 from a local family foundation, and an allocation of $50,000 for site preparation and a small equipment building from the state of Georgia. Southern Technical Institute anticipates that all of the centers can be funded through similar cooperative arrangements.

Another method for acquiring state-of-the-art equipment for engineering technology education is through partnerships with industry. The industries that hire hundreds of highly prepared graduates are realizing that they have a stake in the education of their future employees. They are beginning to provide challenge grants and equipment donations for centers that have the added attraction of being prominently named for the benefactor company. This type of visibility for a company—providing modern equipment in a modern lab that carries its name—encourages other companies to accept the challenge of setting up a lab.

As important as these partnerships are, however, state governments must recognize their obligation to keep instructional labs in state-supported colleges current through annual, predictable equipment allocations in the budget. Indeed, the need is so great at this moment that states should begin with some catch-up allocations.

Apart from developing partnerships with industry and working for better public funding, colleges can also obtain high-tech equipment by charging special fees or higher tuition in high-cost programs. The narrowing of course offerings and curricular specialty areas permits instruction with less (and presumably more modern) equipment. If local needs require a breadth of offerings, however, field trips to industry, a co-op program and industrial internships for students, and visiting lecturers can all reduce the need for maintaining the very latest equipment.

RECOMMENDATIONS

1. The availability of computers and computer technology should be recognized and applied in all academic programs in engineering technology.
2. Computers and computer-aided instruction should be recognized as one of the most powerful educational delivery systems now available.
3. There should be greater inducements to have faculties use modern educational technologies in teaching.
4. Institutions should plan to develop a limited number of "centers of emphasis" in subspecialties.

9

Allocating Resources for Engineering Technology Education.

The early and middle 1970s were difficult times for both engineering and engineering technology education. Enrollments had declined substantially from their peak in 1966, the multiple job opportunities for graduates that had been the rule seemed to evaporate, and available funds for laboratory renovation and new equipment were much less than what was needed. These problems were particularly evident at independent colleges and universities because of their dependency on tuition income. The period saw the development of crises that have persisted, gradually becoming the status quo.

One crisis, the urgency of upgrading laboratory and shop equipment, was heightened by the later upturn in enrollment. Educators were able to call attention to the substantial need for laboratory development, a need that was intensified by a national emphasis on high technology. The public was confident that the nation's role as a leader in the development of high technology would open new resources for prosperity, as indeed it has. Nevertheless, the United States continues to depend on agriculture and other basic industries, industries that often deal with so-called "low" technology, such as welding, foundry, and building construction. In this context and in the discussion that follows, "low technology" is intended to imply the *users* of high technology compared to "high technology" industries as the *producers* of high-technology equipment.

PLANNING

Wentworth Institute offers an example of the type of planning for both high-tech and low-tech engineering education now being used by many institutions. In 1975, a group at the institute completed a general planning document of goals for enrollment, new programs, faculty, and faculty development. The exercise did not designate laboratory and shop development as either high or low technology. (However, almost 10 years later, out of 10 areas of substantial refurbishing and development, 5 are low technology and 5 are high technology.) As planning proceeded, the dilemma of limited resources and unlimited claims on these resources remained. The impact of any allocation of financial resources on the academic programs required consideration. An arbitrary rule of thumb was used to maintain support in two major areas: half of available funds would go toward the renovation and upkeep of buildings and utilities, while the other half would be used in the classroom and for laboratories and shops. This funding formula is also flexible, however, and varies from year to year as resources and needs change.

BASES FOR RESOURCE ALLOCATION

For any institution there are various motivators in the allocation of resources and a number of factors must be considered. For example, as a way of dealing with in-house politics, it seems desirable for everyone to get something, but this may spread resources so thin that their impact is minimal. Indeed, the result may actually be negative if large numbers of people feel they did not get what they deserved.

The strategy of rewarding and building on strength is a conservative way to ensure the role of leadership by certain departments within an institution. Many believe it reasonable to expect that the best departments have the best claim on added resources. However, this notion does not leave room for the advocate of new programs and laboratories.

In addition, some thought must be given to community needs as well as to the desires of the students. In the New England area, for instance, there is a continuing industrial need for engineering technicians in the areas of industrial engineering technology, manufacturing, machining, and welding although these programs are less popular with students. (Students are currently flooding computer software courses.)

LOW-TECHNOLOGY AREAS

Institutions must decide how to allocate their resources within the categories of low and high technology. In the case of Wentworth, there are five areas of low-technology study: precision measurement, welding, foundry, building construction, and internal combustion engine laboratory. Although it is true that a great deal of high technology has been used in these areas with new knowledge being generated every day, study at the undergraduate level should give the student a good grounding in the basics of these fields and some feeling for what high technology will do for them. These five low-technology areas are discussed below.

Precision Measurement

The Precision Measurement Lab allows instructors in the machine shop to measure length precisely in a temperature and humidity controlled atmosphere and to introduce the vocabulary of precision measurement, a vocabulary that can be carried over to the measurement of any characteristic. Precision measurement is important for engineering technicians. Learning how to measure length allows greater understanding of the measurement of temperature, pressure, voltage, current, and the various derivatives such as velocity and acceleration.

Welding.

Years ago, welding was generally added in the corner of the foundry in many manufacturing plants. This was also the case in technical schools, but gradually instruction in welding increased while instruction in foundry activities declined. (This reversal was also reflected in the demand for graduates in these two areas.) Introductory welding courses still include the traditional gas and arc welding activities; however, Automatix robot and a variety of automatic inert gas-machine welding experiments are also part of the curriculum. In addition, whereas cutting formerly was done exclusively by oxyacetylene, now plasma cutting arcs slice through multiple layers and high conductors such as aluminum and copper.

Foundry

Grey cast iron foundry work was included in college curricula until about 1970. At that time, new environmental regulations made it nec essary to dismantle the cupolas, which simply produced too much smoke. Foundry work continued, however, using aluminum and the bronzes. In addition, pattern making was an integral part of the foundry course. (Today the craft aspect of pattern making has virtually disappeared from academic programs because the patterns took too long to shape and finish. Unfortunately the new knowledge that might have increased the speed of pattern making and kept this skill in the curriculum was never provided.) As foundries were remodeled, safety, cleanliness, and eliminating emissions to the atmosphere received major emphasis, reflecting the same concerns that were being addressed by industry. (Indeed, one of the goals of engineering technology curricula is to teach students, by means of this foundry experience, the importance of cleanliness to help them in related activities when they go to work.)

Building Construction-Carpentry

Although one sees new types of machines in new carpentry laboratories, there are none that could be called high-technology equipment. Even the instruments that read moisture content in the lumber were available in the mid-1940s. Nevertheless, building construction-carpentry is still an important low-technology area (this shop is one of the busiest places at Wentworth), supplying graduates to major, midsize, and small contractors for all levels in operations and management.

Internal Combustion Engines

Internal combustion engine courses are modified when new engines, instrumentation, and load banks are obtained. Engines are instrumented with a variety of temperature pick-ups and flow meters wired to computers. In this case, then, high technology has entered a laboratory devoted basically to a low-technology activity.

HIGH-TECHNOLOGY AREAS

Institutions can divide their high-technology program resources in a variety of ways. At Wentworth, for example, the five laboratory areas that reflect high technology are the printed circuits laboratory, the physics laboratory, the computer center, the computer hardware laboratory, and a numerically controlled machining laboratory. These areas are discussed in the paragraphs that follow.

Printed Circuits.

Students in a printed circuits laboratory begin with a schematic diagram; approximately 100 steps later, they are ready to test a completed printed circuit board. All of the components are mounted, and the board is packaged. Current projects at Wentworth include a two-channel audio amplifier, a digital clock, and an auto-alarm system. Printed circuits labs include the photographic process equipment needed to make the masks; imaging, developing, and photo-etch equipment needed to develop the board; the microdrilling equipment; and the soldering apparatus. Such laboratories reflect the major activities of modern printed circuit board manufacturers.

Physics Laboratory

Physics is an extremely important area for all engineering technicians, and the laboratory must be in keeping with what one will find in industry. The temptation is to leave the introductory physics laboratories unchanged because the theory and practice of what is done at the undergraduate level was probably well established prior to the year 1900. However, measurement techniques, such as using strobotacs and laser beams, have changed.

Computer Center Facilities

As engineering technology institutions continue to expand, computer center facilities become more and more important. The computers are used by both students and faculty in academic programs and also by the institution's administration. (The computers can often be used simultaneously by these various groups, but because of added student loads, more administrative work is done in the early-morning hours.)

Computer Hardware Technology

A recent addition to the laboratories at technical schools is a computer hardware technology laboratory. In this lab, students learn to use small computers to enhance and improve technological processes. They experiment with a variety of sensors that provide analog signals that are digitized and possibly multilexed and then processed by the computer. (In some cases, programs have been written so that a digital signal can be sent to the digital-to-analog black-box, which in turn gives an analog signal to drive some activator.)

The equipment is primarily electronic in nature, but the sensors also include devices that measure such variables as linear and rotational velocity, strain-gauge outputs, pressure, and other readings important to civil and mechanical engineering technology. To master this technology, students must learn to use and understand not only applicable software but also the items of digital hardware.

Numerically Controlled Machining

Because of increased interest in computer numerically controlled (CNC) and numerically controlled (NC) equipment, laboratories and technical schools are being developed that are fully dedicated to numerically controlled machining. Although the machining itself can be considered low tech, emphasis is placed on the design of machine parts (to take advantage of numerically controlled machining) and the actual operation of the NC machines.

CONCLUSIONS.

As an example of these activities, Table 4 lists the laboratory and shop areas at Wentworth, the square footage of each area, the space refurbishing cost, the dollar cost of new equipment, and totals for each of these categories. This renewal is part of a program that was begun in 1975.

TABLE 4 Wentworth Institute of Technology—Renovation and Equipment, 1975–1983

Laboratory/Facility	Area (square feet)	Refurbishing Cost ($000)	Equipment Cost ($000)	Total Cost ($000)
Precision measurement	375	25	5	30
Welding/shop	5,500	110	125	235
Foundry/sheet metal	3,700	30	6	36
Building construction-carpentry	10,400	120	25	145
Printed circuits	5,100	178	130	308
Physics	3,200	20	30	50
Computer center	1,600	90	730	820
Internal combustion engine	2,400	35	40	75
Computer hardware	3,600	194	126	320
NC and CNC Machining	1,200	5	160	165
Totals	37,075	807	1,377	2,184

When considering changes in engineering technology education, it is important to remember that low-technology, or "smokestack" industries still provide a major portion of the employment for technology graduates (although some students do go directly to high-tech industries). Because of the interdependency of high and low technology (i.e., low-tech firms use high-tech equipment) students of engineering technology must also understand and be prepared to use high-tech equipment and processes. Engineering technology programs that prepare students for both of these areas—low and high technology —will serve their graduates most effectively.

RECOMMENDATIONS

1. Continuing efforts should be made to upgrade laboratories and shops, recognizing the importance they play in the education of engineering technicians and technologists.
2. Linkages with industry should be developed to share specialized laboratory and shop facilities both in industry and on the campus.

Notes

1. L. F. Smith and L. Lipsett, *The Technical Institute* (New York: McGraw-Hill, 1956).
2. R. C. Mallonee, "An Historical Analysis of Major Issues and Problems in the Development of the Baccalaureate Degree in EngineeringTechnology."Dissertation. (University of Washington, 1979).
3. Accreditation Board for Engineering and Technology of the *Fifty-first Annual Report* (New York: September 30, 1983).
4. Ernest R. Weidhass, "Who Speaks for Engineering Technology?," *Engineering Education,* May 1981, pp. 753–756.
5. National Institute for Certification in Engineering Technologies, *NICET Certification Programs* (1984 ed.)
6. L. Douglas Smoot and Michael R. King, "Engineering and Technology: Differences and Similarities," *Engineering Education,* May 1981, pp. 757–760.
7. *Engineering and Technology at Purdue: Comparison Guide, Schools of Engineering and the School of Technology* (West Lafayette,Indiana: Purdue University, 1980).
8. Lawrence J. Wolf, "A Comparison of Mechanical Engineering and Mechanical Technology Curricula." Paper submitted to the ASEE Gulf Southwest Section Annual Meeting, Louisiana Tech University, March 17–19, 1983.
9. Kenneth A. McCollom, "Programs in Conflict: How One School Tackled the Problems," *Engineering Education,* May 1981, pp. 761–764.
10. Lawrence J. Wolf, "Graduate Education in Engineering Technology: What are the Real Issues?," *Engineering Education,* May 1982, pp. 808–811.
11. M. T. O'Hair, *A Master's Degree in Engineering Technology* (Indiana University, 1982).
12. Wentworth Institute of Technology, *Student Handbook, 1983–84,* p. 18.
13. National Commission for Cooperative Education,Cooperative Education —A National Assessment: Executive Summary and *Commentary* (Boston, Mass.: undated).

14. Engineering Manpower Commission of the American Association of Engineering Societies, Inc., *Engineering and Technology Enrollments, Fall 1983, Part II. Technology.*
15. P. A. Saetler, *History of Instructional Technology* (New York: McGraw-Hill, 1968).
16. Stanford University Institute for Communications Research, *Educational Television: The Next Ten Years* (Palo Alto, Calif.: 1962).
17. Carnegie Commission on Higher Education, *The Fourth Revolution: Instructional Technology in Higher Education* (New York: 1972).
18. State University of New York, *Television in the Classroom* (undated).